"*Freedom of Expression*"

Food for thought
Humorous
Inspirational
Prose
Poetry
Romantic

Gerald E. Raulston

Copyright © 2006 by Gerald Eugene Raulston. 34120-RAUL
Library of Congress Control Number: 2006905223
ISBN 10:   Softcover   1-4257-2100-1
            Hardcover   1-4257-3042-6

ISBN 13:   Softcover   978-1-4257-2100-8
            Hardcover   978-1-4257-3042-0

This book was printed in the United States of America.

design by: chicklet

To order additional copies of this book, contact:
Xlibris Corporation
1-888-795-4274
www.Xlibris.com
Orders@Xlibris.com

I was born in Worden, a small country town in Illinois. I lived there until about the age of ten. My family then moved to another even smaller town about five miles away. There were only two streets in that town.

I attended several schools before graduating from Edwardsvile High School in the spring of 1964.

That year I volunteered four years of my life to serve in the Marines. I am proud of that service and of my country.

I worked for thirty-two years for the same company before retiring. I retired at the age of 53.

I have always liked to express myself. I have jotted down many thoughts over the years.

I look at life and write about it from this point of view, "Wouldn't it be nice if life was this way?"

I think that life is more enjoyable when you try to think of things that make you smile.

I have never considered myself a writer. I think of myself as an ordinary man that enjoys putting into words my thoughts about and some of my experiences in life.

I hope that my writings will be more enjoyed and that the words expressed will move the hearts of those that read them.

I wish to dedicate this book to my family and close friends that have encouraged and inspired me to write.

A special thanks to my daughter, Connie. She has always motivated me and given constructive help. She has continuously motivated me, even when my spirits were down.

Without the words of encouragement from all those wonderful people that helped keep my spirit alive, without them, this book would have never been written.

This book "Freedom of Expression" is in part the works of all those that have supported me.

A special thanks to my family and friends.

INDEX:

THE PRICE OF FREEDOM

Is it thunder or more bombs? I no longer can tell. My senses have dulled and I feel I will soon be going home.

I am doing my best to keep alert and yet my mind drifts. I think of all the past wars that were fought. I think of the many who have laid down their lives in defense of the ideals and principles our country so proudly stands for. Countless numbers of young and old, men and women alike who believed, fought and died for what they felt was right.

The shelling is getting closer and closer. I feel the ground trembling, or is it just me? I think of the killing and how difficult it is on all of us here, as well as our loved ones we have left behind.

Our country has always stood and fought on the side of what we thought to be right. Many times our flag has been ripped and torn but yet through the fire and smoke our flag has stood to the test. Seeing our colors wave makes me proud to serve with pride for this land of the free.

The ground now trembles even more. The screams I hear I am unable to understand.
I feel a intense pain, a pain such as I have never known before. A tearing burning pain. I try to cry for help, but my cries I can't hear over the ringing in my ears. The fighting rages, now the enemies of injustice and fear are upon me. My mind is fading. I'm drifting into a sea of black. The sounds of war cease and the pain I once felt,
I feel no more. I can no longer see.

I know now that I have done as many proud and brave warriors have before. I gave my life for your right to be free.

A season

A Season for Love

Love is all powerful it seems to me.
Enduring love is strong like the mighty oak.
Everlasting love is flexible like the branches of the
willow tree.
It is what is felt in the heart that transcends all
boundaries.
The boundaries from oak to willow and back again.
The winds of life will blow and the willow will bend. Yet the mighty oak
will stand and endure to the end. Love itself is nourished by the light of
forgiveness,
and fed with the seeds of understanding.
A loving heart is fragile and easily hurt, even broken
when not watered with understanding and compassion.
Love is continuously tested through life's seasons of
storms.
The heat of anger, the winds of change, the snows of
bitterness,
The tremors of disappointment, and the pitfalls of
doubt.
For love to survive in our lives,
it must be based on what we feel, not what we see.
If life itself is a season,
then let life be a season of love.

for love

THE POTTERS HAND

A desire to feel whole.
A need to know.
Will the potters hand today
finish his work of clay?
A hurting that never ends,
a burning deep within.
Time is ticking away.
Will the sun set another day?
A passion to feel alive.
A burning deep inside.
A burning love to share.
A love for one that truly cares.
I have found the missing piece,
now within I have peace.
Time is ticking away.
The potter has finished his work of clay.

Gerald E. Raulston | **11**

ANGEL OF MERCY

As young children, strong, full of life and overflowing with energy.
Life was enjoyable, worth living. They gained satisfaction from doing and giving.
Through many accidents they would go, always coming out smiling and ready to go.
Through many mistakes and misgivings, they never had a desire to give up on living.
Now their lives are becoming shaded, their desire to live has faded.
Their bodies are changing and slipping from light.
The pain drains them of all their might.
What once was will never be.
Their window of life is slipping into eternity.
Once standing, proud and strong.
Now it is a struggle to simply get along.

They pray for the Angel of Mercy that comforted them, to give way to the Angel of
Death, and let them rest.
There once was a time of fear,
a time they feared ascending from here.
The Lord gave them life through his love,
now they pray daily for mercy from above.
Within, they feel the Death Angel now lives. They feel they have given
all they can give.
They once were filled with a desire to live,
now they have lost their will to live.
They pray to God and all his mercy,
to give them peace and let them rest.
Soon the Death Angel will sing their song, and in a blink of an eye they will be gone.
In our minds and heart their memories will remain
until that day when we will be together again.

innocence

INNOCENCE

Through love a child is conceived.
Now a child is soon to be born.
The time, name and place,
is not important.
A child soon to enter our world.
Free and innocent it will be.
Knowing nothing,
not even where he might be.
The foundation of his being depends
on what he sees and hears us say and do.
Care must be taken,
in the examples we give.
For if they are wrong
the child's innocence will soon be gone.
Now you plant the seeds of knowledge
and you hope to see them grow.
Soon it will be time
for you to step aside,
to let him take his place
in the world outside.

Gerald E. Raulston|*13*

kissed by

KISSED BY AN ANGEL

Caressed by gentle hands,
drawn close.
Eyes sparkling like diamonds
in the moonlight.
Lips, soft as silk,
moist, like the pedals of a rose in the morning dew.
Closer and closer,
heat radiates between.
Lips touch.
No words need spoken.
From an Angels lips
is felt an unforgettable kiss

SPECIAL

How do I know,
that you are "Special?"
It is my heart that tells me so.
I know that I would walk through fire,
wind, rain, and snow if it would
make your heart smile.
Wishing only that in your tender heart
that there would be a little place for me.
I know in my heart
that you are so "Very Special."
Always remember,
"All good things come from the heart.".

Gerald E. Raulston |

A MONET OF WORDS

To search for and never find
is like living blind.
To look for but unable see
is like being a piece of coal cast deep into the sea.
By chance something beautiful has happened,
like the stroke from Monet's brush.
The piece of coal, all weathered and battered about,
is left alone on the shore.
To search and never find.
To want and never know.
Then he saw that piece of coal.
He held it in his hands, rubbing away
the horrors it had endured.
His hands now open, what he has is not a piece of coal.
In his hands he held a diamond.
He knew that one day his search would end
and he would feel what perhaps was destiny.
He searched. He found.
Now a special happiness dwells within.

THE SERPENT'S TONGUE

Outward appearances of Christian love sometimes cloaks
the inward dwelling of the Serpent's tongue.
Words of goodness and trust
tainted by ill thoughts from twisted minds.
Honor and respect lost or questioned,
because of the Serpent's tongue.
Faith and calmness of mind
triumphs over wicked words.
Thoughts of distrust breaks the heart.
Eyes swell with tears of pain.
Prayers said and forgiveness declared.
The Serpent's tongue speaks no more.
God's love and guiding hands
strengthens the heart.
Gentle words, heavenly sent,
dries the tears of implied shame.
The Serpent's tongue now silenced.
God's love overtakes. .

ANGEL BY MY SIDE

Day by day I seem to be drawn in different ways.
I try to do what I feel is right, but yet
things turn out wrong.
Easy it would be to give up and give in.
Easy it would be to fall
into a life of self indulgence and sin
On my knees I pray
asking God to light my way. I ask for guidance
and a sense of purpose and worth.
As if by magic I now see
and come to know the power of Thee.
An Angel appears for my eyes only to see.
To others my Angel is like you and me.
Her words of encouragement seem heaven sent.
Now in times of trouble and despair
my Angel is always there.
Once I felt doomed
to sink into sin.
Now my Angel
is my very best friend.

Gerald E. Raulston | 19

TALK WITH ME

You are always there,
like the stars above.
Your heart is full of understanding,
compassion, and love.
You give hope
in times of despair.
You give an inner strength
beyond compare.
You say "Accept life,
and ask not for change."
You speak words of honesty and truth,
and to some that is strange.
Your lips speaks words of wisdom.
You create the need for words
not yet written.

Gerald E. Raulston | **21**

TRUST IN PRAYER

Dear God.
Dear God I pray.
Dear God,
take my burdens away.
I feel my love
is like a pearl turned to stone,
cast overboard, sinking
into an abyss of eternal darkness.
Though my heart is warm
because of the friendships I share.
Still my heart feels hollow
in the absence of a love I once
shared.
I fear never to see the twinkle
of heavens light.
I fear never to feel the warmth
of true love again.
Dear God.
Dear God I pray.
Dear God please,
take my burdens away.

RAINBOWS, CASTLES AND MORE

I would like to capture a rainbow
and put it in my heart, so that
anytime you wanted,
you could touch it and feel
the love I have for you.
I would like to build you a castle
that you could call your own.
A place of serenity, warmth, and happiness.
A place where you
would never feel or be alone.
I would like to be the one
who is there if ever you are
lonely or troubled
or just need someone
to hold on too.
I would like to do all this and more
if it would make you happy.
Sometimes, it isn't easy to do
the things I would like to do,
or give all I would like to give.
So, until I learn how to
catch a rainbow and build a castle,
please allow me this.
Let me hold you in my heart
and let me shower you with my love.

true
love

TRUE LOVE NEVER DIES

No one tells you who to love,
for there are no rules from which to play.
You make the rules as life goes on,
learning day by day.
Grief and sorrow may come to pass
but true love will never die.
Individual feelings,
unlike words, they cannot lie..
You are to me, everything,
you are the special reason why.
The life you live, the air you breath,
to feel your joy, makes me cry.
Without you, there would be
no reason to exist.
Life would be a dreary day,
a hazy falling mist.
Remember all the happy times,
and never question why.
Grief and sorrow may come to pass,
but true love will never die.

BEST FRIENDS

By chance a stranger you meet,
a friend to be if you choose.
A good friend to be you hope,
perhaps, one you hope to never lose
You look at him and wonder.
You ask yourself, "Why?"
Why did I ever stop,
instead of passing him by?
You ask yourself,
"What have I done and why?"
You wonder if you should ask him to stay,
or simply say goodbye.
Could it be
the warmth you hear in his voice?
Could it be
that with him is where you want to be?
Time will tell
as time tells all.
Was starting this friendship
right after all.
Our friendship grows stronger
day by day.
In our hearts we have come to know,
that our friendship will never go.
Now as best friends we are,
I feel I was not wrong.
As best friends
we can not be wrong.

best
friends

PRINCIPALS OR PASSION

Through life we go, many times we never really know
whether or not to let our true feelings show.
We ask ourselves, "What is right?"
As time goes on, we often ask, "What went wrong?"
There are times we want what our heart desires.
Our own actions fan the fires.
Our principles tell us to say no.
Our passion tells us "It is OK."
Our principles expect understanding.
Think of the harm unbridled passion could do.
It is best to let rest your personal desires.
Allow your principles to put out the flames of desire.
When you respect one's desires over your own,
it allows you to respect yourself when you are alone.
Our passion makes the blood boil.
Our principles say "Our friendship we will not spoil."
It is very easy to sometimes do wrong,
when we allow our passion to move us along.
When principles are obeyed in the hearts of two,
those principles will allow their dreams to come true.

Surrendered Hearts

To share the feeling of being loved, both must
give all, holding back nothing.
Both must give their hearts and trust
to each other.
Both must take down the barriers that stand in
their paths.
For them to share their love with each other
they must put aside their fears and doubts.
They must live as one through complete trust
and respect for each other.
Only when their hearts melt, and they
surrender to the fires that burn within,
and only when they let their true emotions
flow will their love become true.
Then and only then will they know the true
feeling of love.

ANGELS WEAR WHITE

Angels appear from places unknown, giving promise to life,
hope for the future,
and comfort for the past.
Angels are special and heaven sent. Seldom are they seen.
Still their presence is felt. They soften the hardened hearts.
Words of comfort and wisdom embrace. A warming peace from within.
All and more comes from your Angel. Your Angel that lives within.

DENIAL

The sun sets on our past, and time unfolds our
destinies.
We live in the shadows of morality allowing it to
tell us what we should do.
It is in the recesses of our minds that our
heart sometimes disagrees.
Our peers say for one and only one should there
be a special love.
Our emotions sometimes become mixed and what was
thought to be love for the one turns into simple
desires.
The heart often speaks, it speaks louder than
the voice of morality.
Deep within, the heart knows what truths
reality holds.
The heart knows the special feeling of a
inner warmth that comes from sharing love.
Love is uplifting, exciting and even
dangerous too.
When the love that is given is real, then
too can be the hurt the heart can feel.
The battle of emotions are won and lost in
our hearts and souls.
When love is given and goes unanswered,
the spirit of love is broken.
Through the denial of love our destinies
are altered.

denial

Gerald E. Raulston | 31

forgiven

FORGIVEN

Astray we drift
through weakness of heart.
On our own we try,
and still fall apart.
The burdens of our day
we feel allows us to justify our actions. In the still and calm of the morning
light, our minds focus on actions of nights past.
Realizing the wrong that could have been done,
often to that special one.
On bent knees with a heavy heart,
we ask for forgiveness and a new start.
Forgiveness comes,
as the clouds separate from the sun.
The dawn of a new day,
will send more burdens your way.
Rising from bent knees you feel loved,
you've experienced forgiveness
through God's love.

THE UNBROKEN CIRCLE

The past, yesterday's reality.
The present, yesterday's dreams.
The future, the hopes of tomorrow.
The past, at times littered with bitterness
from verbal stones thrown, or of unfulfilled desires. Reason enough to look
ahead for a brighter tomorrow.
The present, hope of living yesterday's dreams.
The realization that life has no guarantees of
happiness.
As long as we have life there is always hope for the
future.
The future, a place where all hopes are alive.
A protecting haven from verbal stones and unfulfilled
desires.
The future, a place of hope, desire, and happiness.

DRAW FROM ME

Allow my heart to be your well.
Look within and tell me what you see.
If ever there is a time you feel lonely.
I am near, draw on me.
If ever you feel blue.
Draw from me, I am here for you.
Words are only objects for eyes to see.
Words are only sounds for the ears to hear.
My words when you hear or see then written
are a heart felt part of me.
Look into my heart and soul.
Tell me, what do you see?

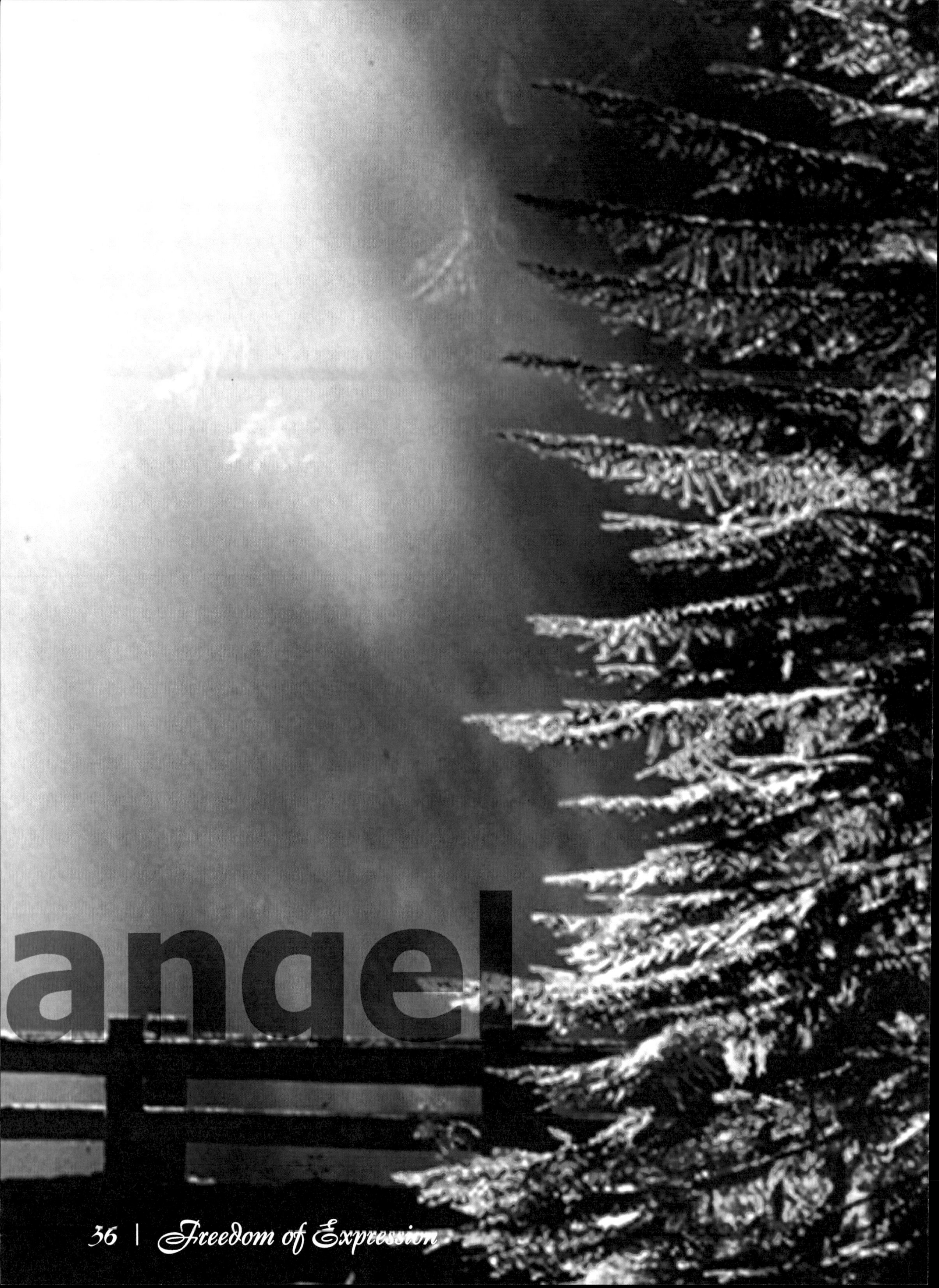

angel

ANGEL

Always there through prayer.

Never forsaking giving comfort.

Guiding the way with loving words.

Embracing touch and inspired wisdom.

Life everlasting through God's love.

i will be there

I WILL BE THERE

When you look and see a bird flying free,
a piece of me is there.
As the sun silhouette the old oak tree,
a part of my soul is rooted there.
When your heart dares to dream,
a lonely part of me will join you there.
As your head caresses the pillow,
your heart knows, I am there.
It is in your heart that I wish to stay.
There is where my heart will rest, I pray.
I will be there, my Love.
I will be there.

SERENITY

At times within our soul
conflicts rage.
It is as if our flesh
is in a struggle against our soul.
As the Lord lets us borrow each breath
it is but another chance.
Another chance to inhale the spirit.
A chance to surrender and let him in.
Only when you let the Lord be your champion of
champions, and your warrior of warriors,
then and only then can you let rest
the troubles that tear at you from within.
We tend to fill our lives with meaningless things,
in doing so we turn our back on the Lord.
We allow our lives to be guided by our desires
in search of temporary happiness.
When you let the Lord live within you
he will make your needs come true.
When you let his love touch your heart
then and only then will the true miracles start.
Conflicts at times will rage within
deep within our souls.
Our souls. will struggle against our flesh
in a struggle for control.
Loving the Lord will bring joy to your soul
and will dry your tears of sorrow.
Your love for him will make you whole.
Through loving him you will gain control.

PASSING OVER

I gaze to the stars,
heaven's lights.
Loved by my family,
and blessed with many friends.
Living each day
to the fullest.
Worrying not of things, I can not change.
Time is short,
this I feel.
I feel a calm,
a peace within.
My Master is calling, now I go to be with him.
Stars now appear,
like sand under my feet.
I look down
and smile.
A loving smile,
for my family and friends.

passing
over

WHO PAYS THE DEVIL

Who pays the Devil and gives him his due?
It is those who are weak and give in.
The victims of doubt and deception
will give in to sin.
Who pays the Devil for tempting you?
It is those of little faith and a weak mind.
The Devil laughs,
as he tempts you.
God's love is stronger than deception.
Shield your body and soul
with faith, and never
allow the Devil to live within.
God's love is free,
yet the Devil's doings has an eternal price.
Turn not to sin,
for in the end the Devil will win.
Who pays the devil?
Who gives him his due?
With God's love in your heart,
it won't be you.

THE HEART SPEAKS

Eyes now closed
thoughts run ramped.
Dreams, wishes and desires stir the blood.
Wanting to bring happiness, not knowing how.
Sorrow is felt, heads now bow. Thoughts of you
give life to my heart.
Wanting to make all things warm and desired.
Your beautiful smile makes me tingle.
Your gentle touch
makes my knees shake.
My tearful eyes answer. No need to speak
My lips are silenced. My heart now
speaks.

YOU ARE MY REASON

You are my princess.
You make me feel like a prince.
You are my angel.
You give my heart strength.
You are the sun.
You brighten my life.
You are my reason.
You are the essence of my being.
You are my dream.
You give my heart a peaceful rest.
You are my fire.
The fire that burns deep within.
You were sent from above. You are
"My Love."

SILHOUETTE

Streaks of lavender and gold
fade with the setting sun.
Shadows of darkened images appear,
as the mysteries of the night unfold.
Alluring sounds of a distant waterfall
beckons your presence.
Majestic pines reach effortlessly toward the heavens
like gladiators, standing proud and tall.
The sounds of darkness are without plan.
The distant footsteps, the rustling of leaves.
Shadows are reflected in the still waters,
the darkened shadows of man.
Hoot-hoot-hoot, the wisdom of the Owl is imparted.
Slowly the mans head is turned upward.
The moon beams capture his joyful eyes.
Clouds roll in, the silhouette departs.
The far off cry of the coyote and whippoorwill
brings to life the still of the night.
Wisps of wind remove the clouds.
Now stands the silhouettes of two.
Their shadows now become as one
as they embrace.
The sounds of wind and passion are heard
as their hearts throb as one.
There is no thought as to what might happen.
The twinkling of their eyes, speaks loud.
The language of their bodies briefly overtakes
as time stands still.
As the night gives way to the light of day,
hearts are happy and fulfilled.
Boundaries were crossed in the shelter of darkness.
Night gives way to the light of day.

A GODSEND

Sad it is when dreams remain only dreams
and tear drops disappear in the sand.
Sad it is when wishes are blown out
like the candle's flame,
and the star's twinkle is shaded by clouds of despair. Sad it would be if we let
others take our dreams away and fill our lives with loneliness day after day.
This will never be, for the Lord is in me.
He has sent an angel to comfort and see me through.
God has sent an angel,
he has sent me you.

a godsend

THE JOURNEY

The darkness of night temporarily conceals
the deception of the world around us.
Mornings early light awakens the sleeping.
The beagles bark, the hounds bay,
the birds chirp, and the dew fades.
The sun ushers in a new day.
What we think we are is not always the picture
our actions paint. We try and sometimes
fall short. We ask for a new start.
When we pass, life is difficult no more.
It is the memory of us
and how we were perceived that remains.
The journey through life requires
giving and understanding of those who
our lives have touched.
Our rewards come from knowing we have done
our best. Sometimes we are misunderstood.
The heart knows of our intended good.
Riches and things of wealth that give
momentary pleasure would be gladly given
for a day of healthy living.
The sun sets at night.
The tides cleanse the shores.
Another day, another chance awaits.

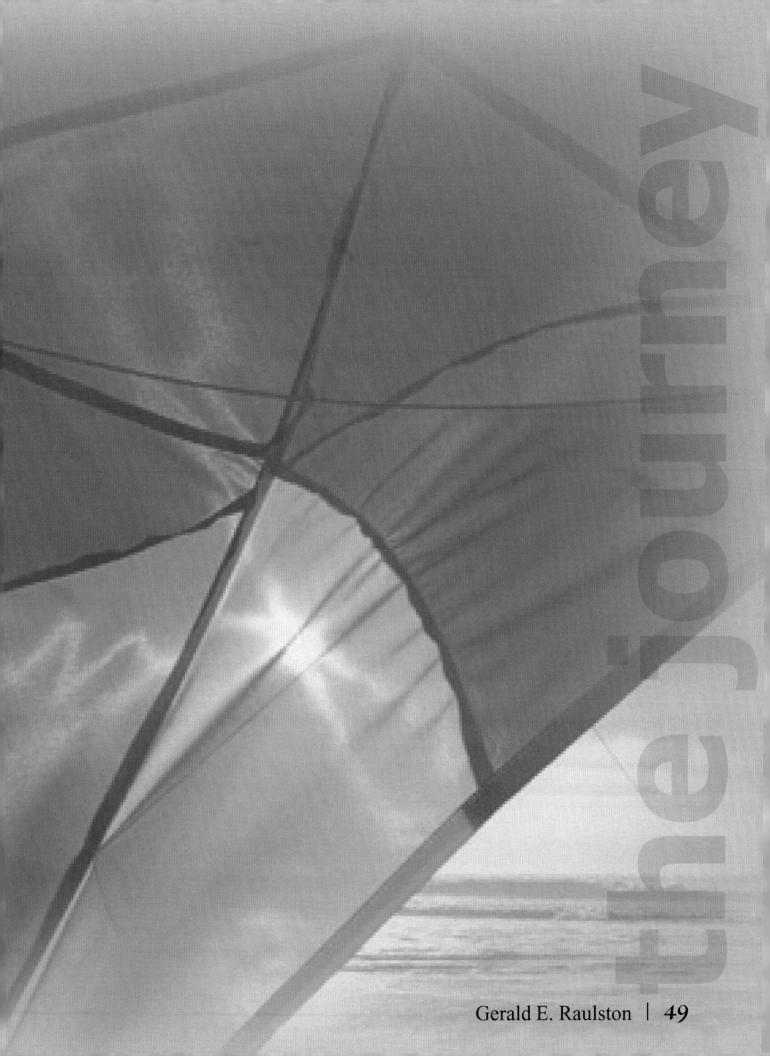

my
strength

MY STRENGTH COMES FROM YOU

A little smile, perhaps a giggle or two from you
is what I need to help me make it through.
You are my Angel, rare indeed
always there with gentle hugs when I am in need.
When the days are tough, and the skies are gray,
what I need is you to brighten my day.
To know you are there no matter what or the reason why,
makes my days so happy, my heart wants to fly.
I always try to make sure you know
that you, my Angel are so beautiful and so loved.
I always want to feel your hugs, and tender kisses,
and to make happen your wishes.
I want you to know that when every day is through,
that my Angel "I Love You".

comes
from
you

A ROSE

You are a rose at its purest. An innocent, sprouting bud.
Still budding, your greatness unknown,
hungering for fullness of life.
As a budding rose in the midst of thorns, you reach out, breaking all
restraints. Prevailing against those who hamper you,
your beauty emerges in all its uniqueness.
You are, as a tender rose, blossoming, petal by petal. Unfolding, becoming
whole,
allowing all to see the beauty of you.

a rose

TO LOVE A BAGEL

A bagel here, a bagel there,
a smile on her face,
and bagels everywhere.
From dawns early light
to the dusk of night,
bagels are her heart's delight.
Apple, cheese, rye, and wheat were always there
but raisin and cinnamon,
are her favorite beyond compare.
With the graceful moves of a dove,
a nibble is taken
from the bagel she so loved.
Her lips close, without a sound.
She rolls the tiny nibble round and round
until that heavenly taste is found
The more bagels she eats, the more she craves.
For just one more bagel
she would work like a slave.
She drifts off to sleep for a good nights rest.
with a smile on her face,
and her bagel held snugly against her chest.

Fuzzy Tails

Squirrels, there were two
full of energy
with nothing to do.
They would run
to and fro.
Just trying to have some fun.
Up one tree
then down again.
Running free.
Find a nut here
bury it there.
It was that time of year.
A frantic scurry
to find a nest.
Winter is coming, and in a hurry.
Snow now falls.
The ground is white.
The night winds call.
Safe from harm
with tummies full.
In their nest they rest,
safe and warm.

Gerald E. Raulston | 55

tra q

TRANQUILLITY

Peaceful moments in the shadow
of the sleeping sun.
Beneath the stars
hours swiftly pass.
The sounds of nature are magnified
as the sea rages against the shore.
Nature calls
wanting to be heard.
The moon briefly breaks
from behind the clouds.
The waves shimmer like diamonds
only to disappear when caressed by the shore.
The tide has come
and now bids farewell.
The moon now sleeps.
The sun overtakes.

IMPRISONED

No bars, no locks, only morality bound.
Hearts are broken, cannot mend,
sake of morality, kept within.
Webs are spun like the spiders home.
Struggles for freedom, useless toil.
The bonds of morality weaved within.
Hopes are dimmed, lights out.
Life's end draws near.
Imprisoned, with fear.
A ray of hope, a shining light.
Morality struggles with the soul.
A struggle for control.
The hearts bleeding, goes unknown.
Life goes on.
A weakened heart, grows cold and old.

imprisoned

TO THY OWN HEART BE TRUE

Beneath the cover of pretense and expectations
lies the need for personal contentment.
Giving up of your expectations
for what others expect.
Rendering happiness to others
sacrificing your own.
Pieces of your heart are torn
like blossoms in a storm.
Your wants and desires are second.
All is given in the name of love.
Search within your inner self.
Time, fleeting moments, to never return.
Turn to your heart
in search of fulfilment and strength.
Your heart knows the desires it conceals,
as it too, know what is real.
Deceive yourself not,
and be not alone.
Step out, reach for what you feel,
and make it real.
Time continues to pass.
To thy own heart be true.

Love is meant to be lasting. Feed it with kindness and understanding and it will grow.

Out-reachings from your own heart, without thought of selfish wants and desires, entrusted freely will kindle the fires of love.

Vows of self dedication and a constant showing of tender feelings, are to be shown through not only words, but also loving deeds.

Emotions as well as a devotion to a special one without a selfish regard to ones own self and a desire to share with and give all are some of the fundamental requirements for the birth of and growing of love.

LOVE

is of no use when it is held within. Held within it will suffocate and die. Love should never be wasted, instead it is to be embraced.

I CAN SEE MY ANGEL

She is standing there,
the warm summer breezes
blowing her beautiful hair.
Her happiness comes from sharing,
a sharing from within
From her heart, all loving and caring.
Her hair, a beautiful soft silky blond
flows freely
as if spun from a magical wand.
She is as light as a feather
with graceful curves that flow
like a gentle breeze in a field of heather.
With capturing eyes of a shade of blue
like the warm tropical waters,
and as soft as the fresh morning dew.
She is my Angel, all five foot three
and with her
is where I want to be.

Gerald E. Raulston 63

THE POWERS OF LOVE

Unbridled love will remove all doubts.
Compassionate love will take away the hurt.
Honest love will erase distrust.
True love will make a house a loving home.
A love withheld is powerless.
Love freely given and accepted is all powerful.

THE RIGHT MEDICINE

For many each day is a struggle
to simply reach it's end.
Only to awaken
and start all over again.
Their will to face tomorrow has left.
Their desire to go on is weakened.
Some call it depression,
others say it is all in the mind.
Doctors will simply say,
take this pill or that.
Do they really know,
or should you believe what they say to be so?
Depression, or is it all in the mind?
They use these words for lack of better ones.
Perhaps it is a temporary loss of focus, rejection,
or a personal loss seemingly impossible to overcome.
The right medicine can be as simple as
taking time to make someone laugh.
It could be a gentle hug
or tender kiss.
Comforting from a loved one, family member,
or close friend, it makes no difference.
Take a little time, show compassion
and listen with an understanding heart.

Gerald E. Raulston | 65

MAMMA'S PRIDE

Awaked from my sleep,
I knew not by what
or even why.
I felt something pulling at my feet.
There were lights so bright,
too bright for my eyes to see.
I knew then
a different world I was in.
I kept my eyes closed,
because I didn't want to see.
I soon opened them and saw
all those giants looking down at me.
From place to place
I went.
From where, to where,
I didn't know.
I took a chance,
and again opened my eyes for another glance.
I knew not what I saw,
but they were all pointing at me.
I came to know,
that there was always one.
With this one,
I would always go.
I thought, "This is not so bad,"
because she was always warm and soft.
In her arms
I felt safe from harm.
When I would cry
she would wipe the tears from my eyes.
She would always feed and hold me,
making me feel warm inside.

When she made these strange noises,
I would look up at her and wonder,
"What was she trying to say,"
"Mama's here," I would hear her say.
Day after day I would hear her say,
strange and different words.
Now, with my Mommy
I learned to make noises and play.
Now, bigger I was becoming,
I would look at her and think,
"She is my Mommy,"
Then she would say, "Mama's coming."
I always made messes
but, she never complained,
even though on her
I must have been quite a strain.
I learned to crawl
and pull at everything.
I would here her say, "No, no,"
and by her hand I would feel a little pain.
I soon learned
to avoid the pain.
I learned to make life
a fun and loving game.
Then one day
I decided not to crawl
instead, I stood up
proud and tall.
I said, "Mommy, Mommy,"
then I saw her cry.
She cried because she heard
her pride and joy say his first words.

Gerald E. Raulston | *67*

a
mid-sum

A MID-SUMMER'S EVE

The still of the night. The moon shines bright.
A need to feel.
A need to know.
Longing to kiss.
The touch of tenderness.
Lying back upon the ground. Moon beams shinning down.
A need to know.
A need to feel.
The feeling of love.
The feeling of being loved.
To feel the touch,
of tenderness upon my chest.
Looking into moistened eyes, that twinkle like the morning dew.
The warmth and tenderness of love. The warmth of sharing love.
Lying down, looking to the stars, in the still of the night.
Love is felt,
through and through.
Hearts are searched,
on this mid—summer's eve.

Dreams

Close your eyes little one.
Journey into a land beyond dreams,
to a place where dreams come alive.
Be yourself.
Open your tender heart.
Let your warmth and beauty to shine.
Allow your emotions to flow.
Weave a tale in your dreams.
A tale filled with emotion.
Open your heart for that special one.
The one who would walk to the end of the earth
in search of you.
Close your twinkling eyes.
Dwell in this place.
In this land where dreams come true.

INSPIRING EYES

Your eyes tell on you, of your deepest thoughts, hopes
and desires too.
Your eyes bring forth warmth and expressions of joy,
promise and hope.
Within all their beauty they tell of despair and the
heartache that dwells within.
Your eyes have a heavenly sparkle as if kissed by the
early morning dew.
Your eyes send forth tears, twinkling pearls of love, a
gift from above.
Your beautiful eyes show and always tell when things
are lovingly appreciated.
Your eyes tell so much on you, they tell of a passion
to love and sorrow too.
Your eyes speak of compassion that is felt within, they
speak without words.
Your eyes are an image of you, they tell of your love
and of all the good you do.
Your eyes are a mirrored image of you.

Gerald E. Raulston | 71

just a
you a

JUST AS YOU ARE

A Countess you could be.
A Queen you are to me.
What you are, makes no difference to me
because I love you just the way you are.
You could be a picture taker
or maybe, a candlestick maker.
My darling, it makes no difference to me.
because I love you just as you are.
You could be rich or poor
neither could make me love you more.
My darling it truly makes no difference to me
because I love you just as you are.
I love you my Darling.
I love you just as you are.

night dreams

NIGHT DREAMS

If my love
could be a diamond,
I would freely give
this diamond to you.
What I hold true
and feel for you
is much more than a dream. It is love, honest and true.
By day I think
loving thoughts of you. By night in my dreams
I comfort you.

A MATTER OF PERCEPTION

If you could look through his eyes and see yourself,
what would you see?
Would the image you see be cloudy or clear, not as in
transparent, but well defined?
When he does something special for you, do you ask
yourself, what does he want?
Do you try to make yourself look better by doing
special things for him?
Do you feel you are always right, and seldom wrong?
Can and do you admit it when you are wrong?
Do you feel that all you do is for the best, or is what
you do simply best for you?
When you look at him, is he really what you make him
out to be?
When he looks at you, what does he honestly see?
When you look into a mirror you see an image that
appears clear.
When you look into your own heart, is your picture
always so clear?
When he looks into your heart, what will he see?
Will the picture be cloudy or clear?

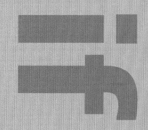

IF

If you were a gem, a diamond you would be. Perfect in every way. Always sparkling and shinning brighter than all others.

If you were a flower, then you would most certainly be a beautiful rose. Fragrant, sweet and soft to the touch. In constant balance, a picture of absolute perfection.

If you were a tree, then a proud oak you would be. Standing proud and firm. Giving shelter to all in need.

If you were a star, then the north star you would be. Shinning bright guiding the way through the long dark nights.

If you were a planet, then Venus you would be. The goddess of love and affection. An example to all of what one should be.

If you were a season, then spring you would most definitely be. Ushering the newness of life. Warming the hearts of all those that know you.

If you were a mineral, then you would be gold. A most sought after mineral because of its fine qualities and value.

If you were a number, then seven you would have to be. Seven, the number that is said to represent perfection, just as you are perfect at everything you do.

You are what you are, "Perfect in every way".

NOW IS THE TIME

If you are ever going to love me,
tell me now, so I will know,
that your sweet and tender feelings,
are true, and you love me so.
Love me now, love me deep.
Don't play with me, then make me weep.
If in your heart you feel for me,
open you heart and give it to me.
Tell me now, tell me true,
tell me if I am the one for you.
Love is not a toy, it is not a game.
Tell me now by calling my name.
The time has come to tell me,
so tell me with your heart felt words,
and show me by your actions too.
Do you truly love me, as I do you?

THE WINDS OF LOVE

The winds of love
are unlike the winds of life.
Winds of the love cannot be seen
but they are deeply felt.
Winds of life
blow hot and cold.
The winds of life
affect you on the outside.
The winds of love burn
like the fire of an internal torch.
Love, like no other feeling,
guides blindly the affections of the heart.
The winds of love bend
but never break.
The winds of love endure
and never forsake.
If not for the winds of love,
then what would life be?
If not for the winds of love,
where would your heart be'?

MASK

Dazzled by what we see.
Our eyes blinded from reality. Looking at but not seeing.
Smiles deceive the eyes
of heartaches that lie within. A longing for love grows old.
Cards are dealt.
Hands are played.
Life goes on.
Pleas, made with out-reached hands go unnoticed.
Darkness falls.
Father Times hand has passed twelve, now rapidly descending.
Life itself near ending.
Innocent flowers die,
their buds never to unfurl, never having graced our world.
Stars fade away,
giving hope.
The sun ushers in a new day.

Live Today

Smell your roses today.
Time is flying by.
The flower that blooms today,
will tomorrow begin to die.
Be not shy, wisely use your time
and make your life full.
You have lived so much,
but there is so much more life to live.
The time to enjoy life to the fullest
is always now.
Time past will never return.
Live today and wait not for tomorrow.
The sun, heavens light,
has reached its peak.
In time it will rest,
and darkness will overtake.

Gerald E. Raulston | 81

BEDAZZLED

Standing in the bright, shinning sun with golden threads of silken hair,
as if a soft halo surrounding your skin so fair.
With words softly spoken,
like an angel's whisper,
comes encouragement and hope from a heart so tender.
Actions speak warm thoughts just as does the silence. Silence speaks
volumes
without pretense.
Unspoken thoughts,
forbidden to reveal.
Dewy eyes openly surrender what the lips conceal.

ANGELS IMAGE

If only through my eyes
you could see.
You would see the pure beauty
I see in thee.
You would feel the unblemished beauty
of your tender heart.
You would sense the passion
and warmth I have held for you from the start.
If only you knew
my heart.
You would know I long to hear
you call me, sweetheart.
Through my eyes you would see
the greatness I see in you.
You fill my heart with a desire
to fill your heart with happiness through and through.

All is well

I looked into your eyes
the doorway to your heart. I looked into your eyes
and saw deep into your heart.
With your fingers so soft, a gentle touch is felt.
A touch that makes
my heart melt.
Upon my cheek
your tender lips did briefly rest. It caused my heart to skip a beat
within my pounding chest.
If I were to die tomorrow, that would be OK.
For with you in my heart, I am alive today.

Whispering Pines

Beyond the majestic ridge
and through the siren valley
there is a special place.
A cabin just beyond the shallow water bridge.
A place where the birds sing and the cat tails grow.
The smell of timbers burning
fills the night air
around the cabin in the valley below.
The tall pines, like sentries in the night
stand guard beneath the moon lit sky.
The weary birds are now asleep
resting from a long days flight.
Whisper like sounds can be heard
as if the shadows were talking.
A distant fluttering of feathers signifying
the occasional arrival of another wayward bird.
In the cabin beneath the whispering pines
lives the keeper of the woods.
She is where she desires to be,
in the peaceful valley of the whispering pines.

Gerald E. Ralston

You

To look at you is to see beyond simply
"beautiful,"
because you are extra special in so many
ways.
Special, from your radiance,
to the way you proudly carry yourself.
Special from your open and honest words,
to your tenderness of thoughts.
Special too, because of your compassion
and feelings for others.
Your beauty is deep,
beyond your outward picture of perfection.
Your beauty comes from within your heart
and transcends the boundaries of pretense.
Words such as "radiance and compassion,"
these are words worthy of you.
Your radiance warms the heart
as does the compassion you show.
You are beyond "beautiful,"
this, in my heart, I know.

WISDOM IS NOT A GIFT

In the mind
is where most battles are lost,
and doubt vanquishes many dreams.
Wisdom will not come from being either
a reader,
or a writer of powerful words.
Wisdom comes from walking
miles in the shoes of others
and learning from it.
Wiser you will be after
the journey is through if
you still have the desire to dream.
Even wiser yet
is the one that takes the steps
that will allow their dream to come true.

BRIDLED

Feelings, emotions, and desires
flow freely from within.
Wantonly they flow, spontaneous,
harmonious, and embracing.
Drawn out by inward thoughts
of outward expressions.
A desires to know the fulfillment of
suppressed wants and desires.
Propelled forward through
feelings of heart felt emotions.
Restrained by respect
and held back through unselfishness.
Seeking a receptive heart
of wanting fulfilment.
Unshackled, to freely give
the unconditional treasures of the heart.

the brook

THE BROOK

The light of day, now sleeps.
Sounds of darkness come alive.
Beneath the Willow, by the brooks edge,
lies motionless, the shell of a man.
Content in the darkness
his burdens momentarily set free.
Dreams of passion and words
forbidden to speak.
Thoughts of tenderness and warmth
come alive as he sleeps.
The night winds blow
gentle and warm.
The Owl keeps a watch on high
as if an Angel standing guard.
Smiles and soft moans are made,
as the shell of the man turns.
A peace within the heart is felt,
due to the memories of that special one.
The darkness is fading,
a new day is soon to be born.
Again, the burdens are heavy,
but the memories gives strength.
Strength from the peace of night
gives a new meaning to life.
The brook trickles on.

Gerald E. Raulston   91

life

Life

What is is not what it once was. What is will not always be. What will be is yet unknown.
The unknown is tomorrow's challenge.

THE TENDER ROSE

Buzz buzz goes the wondering bee
hungering for, but unable to find.
searching for the perfect resting place
of peace and warmth.
Off in the distance by chance
a garden, a rose garden.
Buzz buzz goes the bee.
lighting upon pedals so soft.
Flowing in the gentle breeze,
the bee holds on tenderly, buzz buzz.
Entranced from inhaling the fragrance of her petals
that cover her hidden treasure, buzz buzz.
Thorns abound to protect the beauty
of the tender rose.
Touched by the suns warming light
she unfuris her petals, to the bees delight.
He moves closer, her sweetness overpowers him,
as he fills himself with her sweetness.
Buzz buzz, go the frantic sounds
of the bee, now spellbound.
Darkness falls.
The bee awaits the dawn,
to taste again the sweetness
of his tender rose, buzz buzz

THE TIME HAS COME

No more to hold back.
No more to keep inside.
Past losses and embedded grief.
The spirit reminds the heart.
The time has come.
The time is now.
Lost friends and loved ones past.
Your spirit will cleanse your heart's loving tears.
The time is now to open up.
The time is now to give in.
To shed the bitterness of loss.
To allow love and forgiveness to enter in.
Now is the time to hold back no more.
Now is the time to move ahead.
It is time to let go of the past.
Time to embrace tears of happiness from within.

EXPOSED

Cloaked with jewels and gold.
Appearance of happiness untold.
The heart truly knows,
yet, within it holds.
Life takes all you can give,
still, within dwells a passion to live.
The emptiness of spoken words.
The treasures of words unspoken.
Beneath the glitter and gold.
Beneath the implied happiness.
Beneath it all,
lives a caged and wanting heart.

A NEW BEGINNING

Stand on your own two feet.
Challenge those who say you can't,
and those who put you down. Seek a better day.
Past is past.
What is done is done.
Go forward, move beyond the past.
Reach out, push yourself.
To accomplish great things you must
not only dream but you must act accordingly.
Every cloud doesn't mean a storm.
Time flies. Spend it wisely.
You are full of wisdom. Share it with the world.
Within your heart is wisdom, warmth,
and gentleness yet unshared.
Let it out so others can know the real you.
Nothing is as strong as gentleness or as gentle as
strength.
Sheltered in your heart are great thing.
Open up and let your greatness show.

FOREVER

The sun still shines
even though you are gone.
My memories of you will forever linger near
as though you were still here.
Although you are gone
and we are far apart,
You will always be here
forever in my heart.

forever

Gerald E. Raulston | 97

YOU ARE BEAUTIFUL

You are beautiful
when you walk.
You are beautiful
when you smile.
You are beautiful
even on your worst day.
You are beautiful
in every way.
Your beauty is magnified
in the things you do.
Your beauty is felt
in the words you express.
Your outward beauty is enhanced
by the inward beauty of your tender heart.
You define beauty by everything you do,
and by everything about you.
Many times it will be said
that you are very special and beautiful.
This will be said time and time again, "There is a special beauty in you."

OUR HERITAGE

As we were born, both you and I,
we were born in this land of opportunity.
We grew day by day and learned
what to do and what shouldn't be done.
In this great land of plenty
we take for granted the obvious.
Things like the air we breathe, the water we drink,
and the land that grows our food.
The trees from which so much comes.
The trees in which we used to play are now few.
The spans of the mighty oaks are few and far between.
Where have they gone?
Who is the blame? what must we do?
Once there was a time we could breath deep, and not cough.
What happened to the air?
Who is the blame? What can we do?
The food providing fields of yesterday are now homes and highways.
Our heritage, we have taken it away.
Who is the blame? What must we do?
We blame others, and others blame it on someone else.
If we are to breath fresh air,
if we want to drink and enjoy clean water,
if we want to protect out land, and once again enjoy

the mighty oaks,
then we must share in the blame.
We must do all we can do today
to make tomorrow a cleaner, better day.
We must not assume these things are free, for nothing
is.
The air, water, land, and the trees, these things do
have a price.
When we were born our world was cleaner.
We enjoyed it because our forefathers cared.
It is time for us to do what ever it takes to make our
world a better place.
Let us clean it up so our children will say,
"Today our land is clean because our parents cared".
Our flag proudly flies over this great land of ours.
Let us not blame, but instead work together.
Work together to make our land pollution free.
This can only be done by you and me

our
heritage

Gerald E. Raulston | *101*

WISH UPON A FALLING STAR

Dreams held within
come to pass.
Special moments captured within the soul.
A wish of understanding
of unwritten words held within.
Endearing caress
sealed in time.
Reality temporarily fades under a falling star.
Dreams come alive
from within the heart.
Desires are fulfilled as time stands still.
Shadowed in the dark of night, I wished upon a falling star.

crun

CRUMBS OF LOVE AND TENDERNESS

If you had baked this cookie and it was filled with your love and tenderness,
this cookie would be the best.
The best there ever would be.
If I were to be given the crumbs of this cookie, my heart would hunger no more..

Gerald E. Raulston |

ALWAYS AND FOREVER

If ever you need some cheer,
if you ever need to talk,
remember me,
for I will always be near.
A lot I do not ask.
I only want to see you smile.
I desire your happiness,
for that I would do what ever you ask.
Always in your heart know this to be true,
no matter what troubles life brings to you,
you will always find me here
to comfort you.
Those special words,
"I love you" there is no need to say.
Through your silence
your love is not only felt but it is heard.

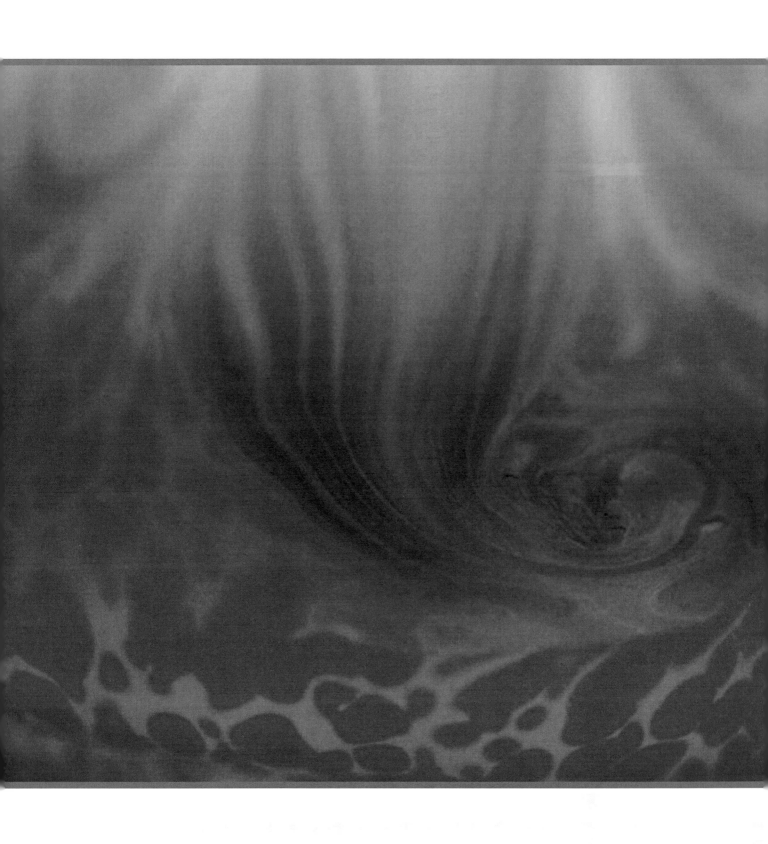

OVERCOMING

The brush flows across the canvas.
Shapes emerge, scattered and vague.
Life, a maze of deception and desires.
Shadows are cast of vengeance and rage.
A picture comes into dominance.
Shapes take on a breath of life.
Words thrown, destructive powers hurled,
transformation, the canvas changes during the night.
Light is shed, the brush covers over,
now imprisoned dreams.
Strength pulled from within overtakes,
parting the bars, releasing imprisoned dreams.
The canvas now covered
with the lessons of life.
The picture emerges ever so clear.
Images of love and fullness of life.

FALLING STAR

Caressed by the dark of night,
the moon and stars shine bright.
I gaze into the distant sky.
A falling star catches my eye.
In the midst of the moon's candlelight,
a wish is made hidden from sight.
A wish for time to stand still.
A wish for my heart to fill.
Desires are felt to be held tight,
on this star-filled night.
From tender lips,
a longing is felt to be deeply kissed.
Wishes are made
upon a falling star.
Dreams were fulfilled
by the light of the moon.

falling star

Gerald E. Raulston | 111

the black

THE BLACK HOLE

Deep within the soul sleeps a motionless void.
A deep dark hole absent of life.
Within the heart lies the keys.
The keys, a means to breathe life into the soul.
The breath of life comes from what the heart sees.
The heart opens and allow love to come in.
Buried deep, deep within the soul,
the heart struggles to breathe life into the soul.
The heart feels. The eyes see
the love that is buried deep,
deep within the soul.

BLIND SIGHT

Even though blind,
I still see in you in my mind.
Your sweetness is embodied,
in the compassion you share.
Even blind, I can feel your tenderness
from the expressions you freely share.
Without my eyes to see, I can sense your happiness
in your cheerful and understanding voice.
Without knowing you my life would be empty,
void of all meaning and purpose.
To know but not see you
is like reading unwritten poetry.
How great it would be to unleash these chains of
blindness and see, even if only briefly.
I desire to see your beauty,
the beauty I can only feel.
To see in your eyes
those unspoken words.
In my heart I hold you close
like a budding rose.
It is in my heart that I see you
and in my heart is where you will forever live.

PASSION

You make my heart flutter and skip a beat.
I am the sand beneath your feet.
My heart pounds with a roar
as I follow you through the door.
We are as one
beneath the setting sun.
Your skin is so soft.
All fear is now lost.
Loving gestures,
passion builds, burning within.
A touch, gentle caress,
You lay your head upon my chest.
Words spoken soft and true,
heartfelt expressions of passion.
Emotional heights reached,
no need to speak.
Together as one
beneath the setting sun.

passion

thinking
of you

THINKING OF YOU

Guided by the warmth of the early morning sun.
The day will not be a loss,
knowing that soon our paths will cross.
I look into your eyes, so beautiful so deep
in search of a sign, a clue,
a doorway to the inner you.
It is with great respect,
and adoration,
that I value every moment I share with you.
As surly as the sun will set,
the time we share
will always be without regret.

"MY HEART BEATS FOR YOU"

Lucky was I
the day we met.
I remember it still
and will never forget.
If you would allow
a song for you I would sing.
A song that would capture your tender heart,
and to your beautiful eyes tears it would bring.
I would sing a song of you my angel.
You are the angel that makes my heart beat.
Your eyes sparkle like diamonds kissed by the morning
dew.
For you my angel there is nothing I would not freely
do.
I would sing my song.
I would sing it loud and clear.
I will sing it to you my dear
and for all the world to hear.
If you could feel the chanting beat of my heart
you would know its words.
You would know that they come from deep within my
heart.
Close your beautiful sparkling eyes
and feel the words of my song.
Put your hand on my heart and feel the words
as my heart sings your song.

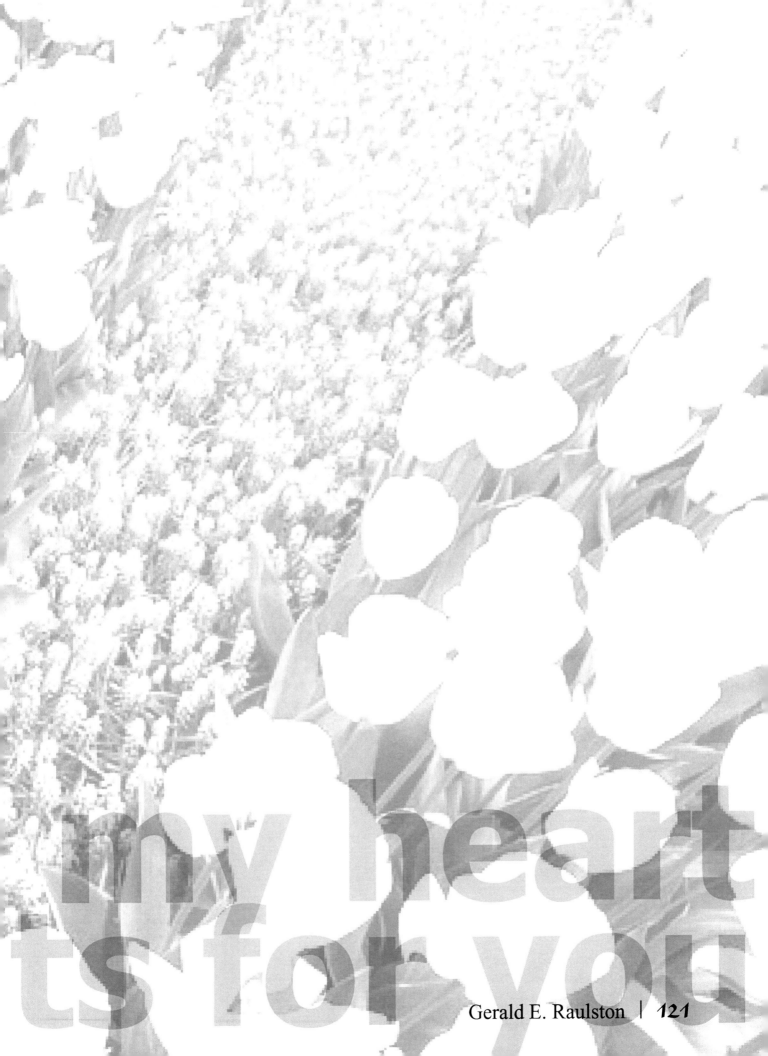

my heart
ts for you

A KISS

Moods, feelings expressed,
emotions revealed.
The touch of soft,
tender, parted lips.
A language of its own,
a kiss brings it home.
To be held in the arms of
the one you love.
To feel the compassion
of what lies within.
Eye to eye,
the world is locked outside.
To be drawn together
lip to lip.
The feelings of warmth and desire
flow without words,
Storms may rage.
The power of a kiss will can silence the rage.

a kiss

A HUG FROM THE HEART

Tenderness, expressed with out stretched arms.
Cradling, giving refuge.
Reaching out with tender understanding
and compassion.
Holding with strength. Compelling a soothing calm
from an understanding heart.
No words need be said or excuses made,
in supporting arms.
Relaxed now. Feeling no fear.
In out stretched arms, shedding happy tears.

NO NEED FOR WORDS

They stand there.
The spoken words have silenced.
Their eyes now meet,
inviting, searching deep.
Hearts beating fast.
Closer they move.
Eyes sensually embrace,
searching, beckoning.
Closer still they come. The hearts of both are throbbing.
With love and passion
his finger touch her soft skin.
Their eyes still entranced,
not even a blink.
Her lips now slowly part, like the petals of a budding rose.
Their eyes close.
Their lips embrace.

for words

COME TO ME

Come to me, my Love,
and fill my arms with your tenderness.
Come to me, my Love,
and hold me like no other.
Come to me, my Love,
let me inhale your sweetness.
Come to me, my Love,
and let me taste you tenderness.
Come to me, my Love,
and remove my haunting feeling of loneliness.
Come to me, my Love,
and fill my emptiness.
Come to me, my Love,
and let me love you.
Come to me, my Love,
come to me.

The Beauty of A Woman

The beauty of a woman is not measured
by the clothes she wears.
It is not in the figure she carries
or the way she combs her hair.
The beauty of a woman must be seen
through her eyes. Her eyes are the doorway to her
heart.
Her heart, a place where kindness, love, and passion
reside.
The beauty of a woman is not simply measured by the
beauty of her face.
Her true beauty is found
in the deep within of her soul.
A woman's beauty is reflected through the care
she lovingly gives and the passion she openly shows.
The true beauty of a woman
grows with the passing of time.

a woman

COOL WATER CREEK

I
remember the times
I played all day
chasing after little rabbits,
only to have them run away.
I can still feel the water on my bare feet as I
played in the cool waters of the creek. In the clear,
rippling water there would be
crawdads, darting away from me.
I would try to catch them
only to slip and fall in.
I can still hear the calling of my fathers voice,
it was time to come in, he gave me no choice.
The sun was setting, no more time to play,
I smile now as I remember
the fun I had
when I had time to play.

THE BEAUTY WITHIN

To look and not see is often reality.
There are those that stare blindly and cannot see.
It is from the heart that goodness and beauty starts.
It is from the heart
that tenderness and compassion springs forth.
To look at and only see the outward appearance
is shallow.
We must look within, deep within.
Actions and spoken words are only glimpse
of a person's beauty.
It make no difference if it be from a man or woman.
We all have greatness within.
Gentle touches of caring hands.
The expressing words of caring hearts
These are only a few telling signs
of ones true self, hidden within.
Short or tall, heavy or thin,
black or white, young or old,
it makes no difference,
because we are all beautiful in our own special ways

LOVE LIVES IN THE HEART

When you look at me,
Tell me, what it is that you see?
Look at me. Look deep within
and tell me, what do you see?
In my eyes do you see the stresses of reality?
Do you see the hurt that is held within?
Do my eyes tell of the hopes and dreams
and love I have for you?
When you kiss me, do you feel the warmth
that my heart holds for you?
When you let your head rest on my chest,
can you feel my heart as it sings to you?
When you hear my voice,
does it warm your heart?
When you think of me,
do the words "I Love You " live in your heart?
When love is openly shown
the answer to all these questions will be known.
When you think of me, you will know in your heart,
that my love from you lives in my heart.

SPRING HAS SPRUNG

Spring has sprung
when you can hear the buzzing of the bees
and see the buds on the trees.
Spring a beautiful time when
the smell of flowers fill the air
and new life is seen everywhere.
Winter coats of the children are gone,
replaces by shorts and the singing of songs.
The crickets now chirp all night long.
The birds fly to and fro
looking a place to call home.
A place to weave a nest and make it their home.
Spring, a time to walk in the park
hand in hand.
A time to make plans.
The tulips are pushing through.
The rose bushes are turning green.
The birds are singing their songs of spring.
Spring, a time to renew,
a time to reflect,
to push ahead with out regret.
Spring has sprung
and the fields of clover gently wave
in this land of the free and brave.

spring has sprung

THE POWER OF A HUG

It means so much when all seems lost
to feel the warmth of a tender hug.
To be held in caring arms even if only briefly
is long enough to ease the troubled heart.
A child runs to you with open arms.
Your hug gives protection and says "I love you."
With the passing of a friend or your special love
a gentle, assuring hug will ease the pain.
When your eyes tear and your heart is broken,
it can be a loving hug that helps heal the hurt.
A little child's loving arms around her mothers neck
brings tears of happiness to her mothers eyes.
Reach out with caring arms. Hold close and
ask no questions. Just give comfort.
An old man dying from within
reaches out for a caring hug before his time ends.
The breath of life is given and a child is born.
Loving arms hug the child, protecting it from harm.
The powers of a hug. We all need to feel and share.
The giving of a little hug simply says you care.

TRUST YOUR HEART

There is a secret place that only you can go.
A place where your secrets are kept, a place where only
you know.
This secret place where you go
is your heart, the place where your feelings grow.
Listen to your heart, and trick it not,
for in the end your heart, will deceive you not.
Be honest with your heart and it will carry you
through,
and bring out the very best in you.
Your heart knows, trust it when it speaks.
Your heart knows, when your courage is weak.
Harbor not in your heart bad thoughts or feelings,
and trick not your heart into doing wrongful dealings.
With your heart always be honest and true.
Allow your heart to become the best part of you.
Act upon what your heart tells you.
Let your heart show the true character of you.

THE VALUE OF VALUES

We look and want
the biggest and the best. We think we must have
more than the rest.
The value of material things is only temporary.
The values you believe in can make you extraordinary.
Things you buy new
soon become old.
A love valued
will never grow cold.
Possessions of value will come and they will go.
Hold true your personal values and they will never leave you.
Right or wrong,
the choice is up to you.
The values you keep in your heart will be the true value of you.

WHISPERS FROM THE HEART

A tug,
a twinge from within.
A little hug
is needed to calm the wind.
The wind sings
a lonely song.
The heart whispers
as it sings along.
The heart knows
the words to the song.
Expressions of love impart
as the heart whispers the song.
A tug
a twinge from within.
The whispers of love
have calmed the winds.

whispers from the heart

give me

space

GIVE ME SPACE

In this world
we move at a fast pace.
Give me rest.
Give me space.
Things are expected of you to be done.
Done before the setting of the sun.
From all directions demands on you are made. Give me space, I need to
have some fun.
I need space.
Slow down this race.
My search for happiness
is a constant race.
I need time to smell the flowers.
I need time for me.
Give me space
and let me feel free,
Give me space,
allow me time to think.
Slow down this race
before I sink.
Respect my space
and put a smile on my face.
Thank you, thank you,
for respecting my space.

to share

TO SHARE OR NOT TO SHARE

A big juicy apple
you might share.
You happily give a bite
to someone for whom you truly care.
Your heart
you cannot share.
You must give your whole heart,
if it is for that special one that you truly care.
A piece of apple pie,
this you will happily share.
You will happily share a bite with
the special one for which you truly care.
Your love can not be shared.
To give part of your love would be selfish and wrong.
You must give all of your love.
Give her all of your love and you will not be wrong.
Meaningless things can be shared
like a piece of pie or a bite of apple can be given.
Priceless things, like your heart and your love,
can not be shared. They must be totally given.

or not
to share

Gerald E. Raulston | 151

THE JOURNEY OF LIFE

Through the journey of life we all must go.
We don't always know where the road will lead.
We hope the choices we make turn out right.
As we travel the road, we sometimes find our choices
were wrong, but life goes on.
Even though at times we are wrong, we must carry on.
As times passes our hope and expectations rise.
There are times we feel we can do no more.
This is the time to push ahead and open new doors.
When the sun sets today, this day will be gone.
Tomorrow is a new day, a new chance.
Enjoy life to the fullest, as it is meant to be.
Never give up, never accept, always look ahead.
Reach higher tomorrow than you did yesterday.
Be grateful for what you have.
Take nothing and no one for granted.
Your riches are not only measured in money.
The richness of life comes from within,
from your family and friends.
One of the greatest riches you can have is knowing you
are loved and that your love in return is accepted.
Love is the greatest form of richness.
Without love, life is meaningless in the end.
Life is precious and meant to be enjoyed.
Live life through a loving heart everyday.
Today may be your last.
Tomorrow may never come.
Look within your heart.
Make every day a new start.

Gerald E. Raulston | 153

BE AWARE OF THE COBRA

Cobras have fangs,
what a scary sight.
The venomous fangs
will give you a poisonous bite.
They lay in the grass,
and sometimes play dead.
Before they bite
they always flatten their head.
Some Cobras are black,
and some are gold.
Some die young,
and some die old.
Some Cobras prefer to move in the dark of night.
Other Cobras choose to move in the daylight.
You must remember, they all
have a deadly bite.

be aware of

the cobra

Gerald E. Raulston | 155

DREAMS DO COME TRUE

What good are dreams
if you have no one to share them with?
What good is hope
without fulfillment?
What good is a hug
when you have no one to hug?
What good is a kiss
when there are no lips to kiss?
What good is love
when there is no one to share it with?
What good is life
when filled with despair?
The answers to these questions
are simple you see.
It is with that special one,
the answer you will clearly find.
With that special one
your dreams and hopes will come true. It is in the arms of that special one
that a special hug and kiss await you.

come

true

Gerald E. Raulston | 157

FOR YOU

For you my darling
I bared my soul.
For you my angel
I will always be near.
For you my sweetheart
I surrender my heart.
For you my love
I am here.

"Freedom of Expression"